WHAT PEOPLE SAY
ABOUT STORYMAZE

'I absolutely can't wait till another one of these books comes out. Terry is definitely the funniest man in a small part of the southern hemisphere.'
Therese, 10 years, *Yarra-Online*

'Will entertain youthful modern minds accustomed to doing four things at once *and* talking back.'
North and South

'Terry Denton's unique combination of cartoon-strips, rude narrators and pure silliness, has kids laughing as they turn the pages and looking for more when they're finished.'
Sally Murphy, *Aussiereviews.com*

Other books in the **STORYMAZE** series

5

THE MINOTAUR'S MAZE

written and illustrated by

TERRY DENTON

ALLEN & UNWIN

FOR ALEX

First published in 2003

Copyright © Terry Denton, 2003

Allen & Unwin
83 Alexander St
Crows Nest NSW 2065
Australia
Phone: (61 2) 8425 0100
Fax: (61 2) 9906 2218
Email: info@allenandunwin.com
Web: www.allenandunwin.com
Visit Terry's website at: www.terrydenton.com

National Library of Australia
Cataloguing-in-Publication entry:

Denton, Terry, 1950– .
The minotaur's maze.

For children.
ISBN 1 74114 088 9.

I. Title. (Series: Denton, Terry, 1950– Storymaze; 5).

A823.3

Cover and text design by Terry Denton and Sandra Nobes
Set in Helvetica by Sandra Nobes
Printed in Australia by McPherson's Printing Group, Maryborough, Victoria

10 9 8 7 6 5 4 3 2 1

1

WELL, HELLO THERE!
This is a surprise.

I wasn't expecting anyone to turn the page just then. I guess I'll have to stop what I was doing and introduce myself.

I am your Narrator. If you haven't met me before, you're in luck. My job is to guide you through this book. All you need to do is turn the pages and I'll do the rest.

You can manage that, can't you?

OK, then!

Let the story begin.

Our heroes, Nico, Claudia and Mikey are sitting in a crowded bingo hall in a retirement home on Planet Ithaca in the constellation Ionis Major.

There's a bloke up the front calling out numbers and the room is full of senior citizens busily filling in their bingo cards.

'**Legs . . . 11,**' calls the bloke up front.

'Got it,' says Claudia. 'Only two more numbers to go.'

'I've had enough of this,' says Nico. 'Let's get out of here.'

'We can't go now, you moron,' says Claudia, 'I'm only two calls away from a BINGO.'

'I can't believe you are actually enjoying this game!' Nico laughs.

'Listen, dunnybrush-head, it was your idea to come here. So you just have to wait till I win a game. Even if it takes all night. This is your fault anyway.'

'My fault?'

IT **WAS** NICO'S FAULT. IT ALL STARTED WHEN HE WAS WATCHING TV.

'**All the sixes, 66,**' yells the caller.

'Beauty,' whispers Mikey. 'Only one number to get and I'll win.'

'Me, too,' says Claudia. 'And I feel lucky.'

'I can't believe you two,' says Nico. 'I'm getting out of here...'

'**Unlucky for some, 13**,' calls the caller.

'BINGO!'

'What?' says Nico.

'BINGO! BINGO! BINGO! BINGO! BINGO!'

It's Claudia. She is standing up on her chair pumping her fists and yelling at the top of her voice.

Mikey slumps on the table muttering over and over again: 'I was so close. Just one number!'

'You two are weird,' says Nico.

2

'So what do you think?' says Claudia, holding up an envelope from the Jaws of Death bingo hall. She has won a holiday for three at a health farm on a tropical island on the small planet of Knossus.

'It will be fun,' says Claudia. 'Besides, Nico, there is a great surf beach...and some nearby archaeological ruins for you, Mikey.'

The only problem is that the planet Knossus is in the Galaxy 496X, which is hardly next door.

'No way I'm trusting M.I.T. to get us there this time,' says Claudia. 'He always mucks things up.'

'We could walk,' says Nico.

'I think M.I.T is better now,' says Mikey. 'I've been testing him out on some short flights along the beach and he is deadly accurate.'

'Hrrrmmph,' says Claudia.

'Besides, if we want to go to Knossus any other way,' says Mikey, 'it will take 27 light years. So we really have no choice.'

'Let's take a chance on M.I.T.,' says Nico. 'The surf sounds too good to miss.'

'OK,' says Claudia, 'but if he fouls up I'm selling him for pet food.'

'OO,' says M.I.T.

So the Ithacans take M.I.T. out in the open far away from any kind of interference. They all hold him and meditate on their destination.

Together they calmly whisper to M.I.T.: 'Take us to the King Minos Health Farm on Knossus.'

Slowly the three friends and M.I.T. fade away.

PLIK!

10

11

NICO, STOP THAT BOUNCING! YOU'LL WAKE UP THE GUARDS.

BOING!

BOING!

HEE, HEE.

110101.

LIKE YOU TOLD ME... TO THE FRONT DESK!!

AND WHAT ABOUT THE MUD?

EH?

THE MUD? GRRRR!! MUTTER... MUD!!

13

14

WE'RE FREE!

THIS STORYLINE CONTINUES IN ANOTHER DIMENSION.

A

ERE
RE
OU
ING
OW?

B

TO THE FRONT DESK

NOT WITH ALL THAT MUD ON YOU, YOU'RE NOT!

YOU MUST SHOWER FIRST.

DOUBLE HHRRMMPPHH!

4

By the time Claudia finds her way to the front
desk, Nico, Mikey and M.I.T. are already there.

'Where have you been?' Nico asks Claudia,
who is leaning very close to M.I.T. Their noses
would be touching if M.I.T. had a nose.

'Pet food!' Claudia growls at M.I.T.

'0001.'

'Welcome to the King Minos Health Farm,'
says a huge, ugly man dressed in a white
doctor's-style coat.

'I am your host. My name is King Minos and
this is my health farm. These are my staff. They
will make you healthy. We hope you will be happy.
Have a nice day.'

King Minos signs them in, hands out their I.D.
tags and introduces them to an assistant who
leads them to their rooms.

I don't know if you've ever been to a health
resort, but I have. Last year Mrs Narrator and I
had separate holidays. I went to a health resort
for three days of healthy food, fruit juices and
herbal teas, relaxing spa baths, body massages,
long walks in the fresh air and early nights.
Very pleasant.

Mrs Narrator went to the Chocolate Indulgence Resort on Sussonk. Three days of chocolate puddings, chocolate drinks, hot chocolate spas, chocolate mud cake baths, late-night clubbing and karaoke. More Mrs Narrator came home than left.

But that's another story.

Meanwhile time has moved on. We find our heroes relaxing in the hot spring spas having been pampered for several days with ice baths, full body massages, Friesian herb therapies, mud baths, fruit facials, hot wax and polishes, full grease and oil changes, wheat-grass juice drinks, prune cocktails, and alfalfa and roast vegetable dinners.

They couldn't be healthier.

Suddenly Nico launches himself at Mikey and starts chewing on his arm.

'What are you doing?' yells Mikey.

'MEAT!!

I've got to have some meat,' grunts Nico as he takes a big bite of arm.

'Stop that, Nico!' yells Mikey, beating him off. 'But I know what you mean. If I see another bean shoot, I'm going to kill someone.'

'That's why you come to a health farm, you cretinous carnivores,' says Claudia. 'What's the point of coming here if you eat the same stuff as you eat at home?'

'The point is . . . **I've got to have SOME MEAT!!!'** Nico yells. **'NOW!!'**

'Maybe you and I can do something about this,' Mikey whispers to Nico. 'Meet me tonight at nine in the courtyard.'

5

Inside the store, Nico orders ten Haggis Burgers with the lot.

'And some Gorgon Cola,' adds Mikey.

'0111.'

'Take a seat. I'll bring them over to you,' says a very ugly waitress.

Soon she appears at the table with their order.

One of the uglier sights in the universe now takes place, with two ravenously hungry Ithacan surfers attacking and swallowing their Haggis Burgers. Well, that's what the waitress thinks as she gets covered in flying burger pieces.

'Let me guess,' she says. 'You blokes are staying at the health farm, eh?'

Nico and Mikey grunt between mouthfuls.

'0011.'

The waitress leans on a nearby table and starts chatting. But she is careful not to get too close to Nico and Mikey in case she gets hit with more flying food debris.

'So, have you boys been to the maze yet?' she says. 'Have you seen the Minotaur?'

5 ½

'BURP!' splutters Nico. **'Minotaur?** What's that?'

'You haven't heard of Minotaur?' she asks.

'No,' they reply.

'Well,' says the really ugly waitress. 'There's this legend ... '

Rather than have you die of old age listening to the waitress tell this legend, here's a stick-figure version I prepared earlier.

The Myth of the Minotaur
[told entirely in stick-figures]

GRRRRR!

THE CHILD WAS A MINOTAUR. AS HE GREW OLDER HE TURNED INTO A WILD BEAST...

...EATING BABIES, SCARING OLD MEN AND REFUSING TO DO HIS HOMEWORK. HIS FATHER DECIDED TO LOCK THE BOY AWAY.

DAEDALUS & SON
HANDYMEN
INVENTORS
LABYRINTH
BUILDERS
131331

THE KING FOUND A BUSINESS CARD ON THE FRIDGE AND HE CALLED UP DAEDALUS...

...WHO BUILT THE KING A MAZE, OR LABYRINTH, SO COMPLEX THAT NOBODY COULD EVER FIND THEIR WAY IN OR OUT.

AT THE VERY CENTRE OF THIS MAZE THE KING IMPRISONED HIS SON, MINOTAUR.

DAD?

MAZE

'So,' says the waitress, nearly at the end of her long story, 'King Minos keeps his really ugly son locked up in this maze on the health farm.'

'That's a bit cruel, isn't it?' asks Nico.

'Maybe, but you must understand that Minotaur is a really ugly beast. And I mean really, really ugly. King Minos won't let him out of the maze in case someone sees him. That would bring shame on his whole family. So he figures this is the best way. And he does treat him very well. Anything Minotaur wants is instantly brought to him. Food, drink, computer games, puppy dogs, you name it.'

'Airline tickets? A helicopter?' asks Mikey.

'No,' says the waitress. 'The only thing he can't have is his freedom.'

'How do they get all that stuff to Minotaur if no one can find their way in or out of the maze?' asks Nico.

'Good question,' says the waitress moving in a bit closer to Nico. 'Minos knew the secret to the maze, but that meant he had to become Minotaur's full-time carer. Well, he soon became sick of that. So he had a tunnel built under the maze. And then he installed a high-security guard booth at the entrance to the tunnel.'

'High security?' asks Nico.

'Yes. No one can get in or out without King Minos's permission. He employs two of the best guards in the business and entrusts them with the care of Minotaur.'

'Why keep him locked up in the maze?' asks Mikey. 'Why not build a prison instead?'

'Well, I suppose they have all grown to love the maze, even Minotaur. It's the only home he has ever known. I reckon he wouldn't leave the maze even if you forced him. It's his world, poor ugly beast! Speak of the devil . . .' The waitress sighed. 'There's King Minos now.'

'See,' says Nico. 'Even health-farm owners need a Haggis Burger now and then.'

Nico stares at King Minos for some time then he turns back to the waitress.

'Gee, Minotaur must be really ugly if he's even uglier than Minos,' says Nico. 'Because Minos has a face like a melted wheelie bin.'

'What are you talking about?' says the waitress, looking shocked. 'Minos is the most handsome man on Knossus.'

6

Nico and Mikey and M.I.T. wander back to the health farm.

'Those burgers were beautiful,' says Nico. 'Claudia doesn't know what she missed out on.'

'BURP!!' Mikey replies.

I think that means he agrees.

'Who goes there?'

King Minos's really ugly daughter, Ariadne, springs out from the shadows.

'Gotcha,' she says triumphantly. 'And I can smell meat on your breath!'

'No, not meat,' says Nico. 'Just haggis.'

The really ugly Ariadne looks at Nico.

I know that there is a lot of love at first sight in stories, but this time it is for real. Ariadne thinks Nico is the cutest thing she has seen for…um… ever.

On the other hand, Nico thinks Ariadne is the ugliest person he has ever seen, EVER. He's seen better looking Haggis Burgers that fell out the door and were run over by a truck then picked up by a dog who was then run over by a bigger truck which flicked it up into the back of a truck full of haggis offal that dumped it into a swamp of slime.

Now, I don't think she is **that** ugly. But Nico is entitled to his opinion.

As the Assistant Manager of the health farm, Ariadne feels it's her duty to give Nico and Mikey a good talking to and sends them to bed without their supper. But you don't need to know about that.

What you **do** need to know is that about half a page later Nico and Mikey arrive in Claudia's room and tell her all about the maze, the Minotaur, King Minos and Ariadne.

By the way, if you're interested, Mikey has fixed Nico up with a date with the beautiful Ariadne. But Mikey thinks it's better that Nico knows nothing about this at the moment. So I won't tell him!

7

The next morning, Claudia wakes early. In fact, she didn't sleep very well thinking about Minotaur all night. She wants to know more. Perhaps he will prove to be that ever-elusive man of her dreams.

'Ariadne,' she says, catching up with the Assistant Manager in the corridor. 'How can I get to see your brother, Minotaur?'

'Get to see him?' Ariadne hisses. 'He's not a freak show, you know.'

'I didn't mean he was,' replies Claudia.

'He may look and behave like a freak. But I grew up with him and I know what my brother is really like.'

['**A freak!!!**' Ariadne thinks to herself.]

'He interests me,' says Claudia. 'I mean him no harm.'

'No one ever does, until they set eyes on him. Then they can't help it. They stare. Their jaws drop. They shrink away from him.'

'I've seen worse. I've survived Nico for years.'

'But Nico is like Murillion tofu,' says Ariadne. That's a big compliment on Knossus. Tofu from Murillion is considered the finest in the universe. If you're into tofu.

'So you fancy Nico, do you?' says Claudia.

'Maybe,' says Ariadne. 'What's it to you?'

'That's exactly how I feel about Minotaur.'

'Minotaur!' says Ariadne, darkly. 'It always has to get back to Minotaur, doesn't it? What is it with everyone and Minotaur?'

'Hmmm!' thinks Claudia. 'This Ariadne is a bit touchy about her brother.'

'Maybe I can help you get close to Nico,' Claudia suggests. 'And you can help me with Minotaur.'

As the girls talk on, Ariadne's mind races.

'Claudia is very ugly,' she thinks. 'If she can face herself in the mirror every day, then my brother is not going to look so bad to her. If I could get Claudia interested in Minotaur, maybe this could work out well for me.'

Ariadne turns to Claudia. 'OK, let's do it. Meet me outside the door marked Soybean Information Centre in 17 minutes and 23 seconds.'

'In 17 minutes and 23 seconds?' repeats Claudia.

'That's what I said!' Ariadne is a very precise woman. And punctual.

'Great,' says Claudia.

'And bring Nico and the chunky one with you.'

Exactly 17 minutes and 23 seconds later, Ariadne is standing outside the door.

'Soybean Information Centre?' says Nico. 'What is this?'

Ariadne hesitates at the door. Ariadne is about to break a big taboo. But she is sure it is worth it. She opens the door and ushers Claudia, Nico and Mikey inside.

'This is the Maze Security Control Booth,' Ariadne tells them. 'I've lured the guards away. So you have 6 minutes and 48 seconds before they return.'

The room is very grey and metallic. In fact, the walls are painted with shade No. 35, Security Room Grey, the colour preferred by nine out of ten Security Control Booth Design Coordinators. One wall of the booth is completely covered with TV monitors showing lots of different views of Minotaur's maze.

'LOOK!' says Mikey. 'Minotaur's on the monitor.'

'Who's on the what?' asks Nico.

'Let me look,' says Claudia.

'How ugly is he?' asks Nico.

A smile appears on Claudia's face.

'Not as ugly as you, ape-head,' she snaps. 'In fact he's...,' she takes a deep breath,'... gorgeous.'

Claudia is beaming.

'Huh!' Nico scowls. 'Beauty is only skin-deep.'

'That's deep enough for me, cabbage-head,' she replies.

'Ugliness is only skin-deep too,' thinks Ariadne, standing as close to Nico as she dares.

Minotaur Minos is really not too bad looking. You could even say he is handsome. Very handsome, in fact.

Because the people on Knossus are all so incredibly ugly and ugly is normal to them, they think that the very handsome Minotaur is ugly.

Ugly to them is handsome and handsome is ugly. Does that make sense? Whereas, to us, their handsome would be ugly and their ugly would be handsome. It is all relative. And if you have ugly relatives, you will understand.

Anyway, as you may have guessed, Claudia falls in love at first sight.

So that's twice in this story, so far. Sorry about that. But it happens, I tell you!

'Why should Minotaur be locked up?' Claudia thinks to herself. 'Especially when he's such a Murillion tofu.'

A PIECE OF MURILLION TOFU.

8

I probably need to tell you a bit about labyrinths and mazes, and now seems as good a time as any. Are you ready for this?

A labyrinth is a complicated maze. And a maze is a labyrinth. Does that help?

They are both just a network of paths made to trick anyone trying to walk through them. They are supposed to be fun. The sort of thing you do on holidays. People wander around giggling and laughing until they suddenly realise they are completely lost and have no idea how to get out. Then they become anxious, aggressive, violent, desperate, and finally they give up all hope and die.

And, as we all know, this maze is so complex, nobody has ever found a way in or out.

There is a top secret tunnel entrance, known only to Minotaur's father, his 'loving' sister and the security guards. [And a couple of hundred thousand of the good citizens of Knossus. It's a small island, you see, and everybody knows everything about everybody.]

Anyway, Minos, Ariadne and the guards can wander in and out quite freely through the secret tunnel entrance. They are able to pass through the security screen because their genetic fingerprints are recorded into sensors which instantly recognise them. However, should Minotaur ever try to escape through the tunnel, the sensors won't recognise him and will set off a bank of laser beams and howling dogs and air-raid sirens and hungry geese that would deafen an earless dodo on Madagascar.

It would be impossible for an outsider to get into the maze through the tunnel. Even if they could trick their way past the guards, the sophisticated equipment would defeat and immobilise them.

(The maze is also covered in a cloud of mist. This is cunning Magic Myst that King Minos bought from a travelling salesman from the Duryllium Underworld. It stops people flying over and looking down on Minotaur.)

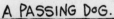

A PASSING DOG.

WOOF!

WATCH THIS.

SSSSPPRAY!

?

HHMMM!!

I'LL TAKE ONE OF THOSE.

WOOF?

ONE? A THOUSAND WOULD BE BETTER.

OK! A THOUSAND IT IS THEN!

The people on Knossus all swap stories about the beast in the maze, but, in fact, very few people have ever seen Minotaur except King Minos, Ariadne and the guards. And now, Claudia, Nico and Mikey.

Not even his mother saw him. Sadly, Minotaur's mother died at his birth, never setting eyes on her incredibly ugly son. Perhaps his sad history would have been less sad if she had.

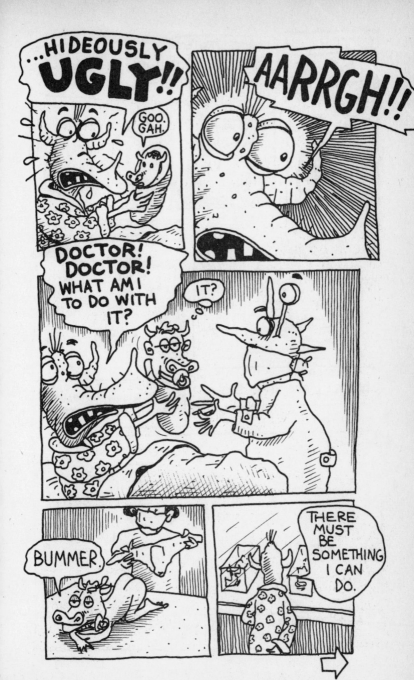

37

LATER:

MY SON, I CANNOT REJECT YOU.

BY PLUTO SHE'S UGLY.

I MUST PROTECT YOU. I CANNOT LET MY IDIOT HUSBAND GET HIS HANDS ON YOU.

I MUST SEND YOU OFF TO SOME PLACE FAR, FAR AWAY.

HIS MOTHER PLACES THE BABY IN A BASKET MADE OF REEDS...

BYE, BYE, MY BABY.

...AND SETS IT AFLOAT ON THE RIVER. IT TRAVELS THROUGH MANY STATES...

COOL!

...AND THROUGH MANY DIFFERENT REALITIES, UNTIL...

38

...UNTIL, DEAR READER, YOU ARE GIVEN A CHOICE OF TWO POSSIBILITIES... TWO FUTURES FOR LITTLE MINOTAUR.

CHOICE ①

HE IS RESCUED BY A BEAUTIFUL QUEEN, WHO HAS NO CHILDREN OF HER OWN.

SHE RAISES THE BABY AS HER OWN. HE GROWS INTO A HANDSOME AND POWERFUL MAN. 'ONE DAY ALL THIS WILL BE YOURS,' SHE TELLS HIM. 'YOU WILL BE KING!'

'BUT I DON'T WANT TO BE KING,' HE SAYS. 'I WANT TO BE A CEILING FAN.'

SO HE STUDIED VERY HARD AND, ON HIS TWENTIETH BIRTHDAY, HIS DREAM CAME TRUE.

OH, JOY!

CHOICE ②

HE IS RESCUED BY A CUTE LITTLE FLUFFY BUNNY FROM HAPPYLAND.

WHO SHOVES HIM IN HER EVIL GOB AND EATS HIM ALL UP!! AND HE IS NEVER SEEN AGAIN. EVER!!

9

Claudia is lying on a bench in the Fruit Suite. Naturally, she is covered with pieces of exotic fruit. Now that she's seen Minotaur, she'll do anything for beauty. She has a piece of kiwi fruit over each eye, a slice of mango over her lips and half a watermelon on the top of her head. And although it's not strictly fruit, she has a sardine sticking out of each ear.

Some exotic calming music wafts through the room, although to Claudia it sounds a bit fishy. Incense sends its delicate aromas through the suite. Claudia's body is totally relaxed. But her mind is hard at work.

'Ariadne says there is no way into this maze and no way out,' thinks Claudia. 'And the most beautiful hunk of manhood in the universe is sitting in the middle just going to waste. Hmmm.'

HMMM, MINOTAUR!!

41

10

Claudia puts the Minotaur down. They are in a hut on an island. The gorgeous Minotaur looks deep into her eyes. They lean toward each other and their lips reach out to...

Suddenly the roof of the hut rips right off and a giant hand reaches in through the opening in the kiwi fruit roof.

Claudia screams:

'AAARRRRGGGG GGHHHHHH!!!!! A GIANT HAND!!!'

Just as quickly, Claudia wakes from her dream, still screaming and rubbing her eyes. The giant hand removing the kiwi fruit roof in her dream was merely Nico, standing beside her, removing the fruit from her eyes.

Claudia jumps to her feet, grabbing Nico by the collar.

'I have to get into that maze,' she yells.

'You mean the Maze of the Minotaur?' says Nico.

'But how?' asks Mikey.

'Simple,' says Nico. 'We overpower the guards, disable the protection devices and storm inside destroying everything and everyone in our way.'

'Yes, but how?' asks Mikey again.

'I can't do it all, Mikey. I've told you how, now you need to work out the details.'

'Quiet, you two soufflé-brains,' says Claudia. 'I've worked it out, and tomorrow you two are going to help me.'

'Who says?' asks Nico.

'This!' says Claudia, showing Nico her fist, close up. 'And this.' She shows him the other fist.

'Oh, them.'

'M.I.T. is going to take us to the centre of the maze,' Claudia announces. 'Where is he?'

'Dunno,' says Nico.

'10010.'

A half a watermelon wobbles toward them. It is the half-watermelon that fell off Claudia's head. And trapped under it is M.I.T.

'Gotcha, you little rascal,' says Mikey.

11

Meanwhile, far away from the troubled life of a simple ceiling fan, dawn arrives on Knossus. Up bright and early, three and a half figures scuttle across a courtyard towards the Minotaur's maze.

CATCH UP.

DANGER LABYRINTH

WHAT IS A LABYRINTH, AGAIN?

QUIET! BLOCK-HEAD.

OK, M.I.T. IT IS TIME FOR YOU TO PERFORM.

110001.

TAKE US TO THE CENTRE OF THE MAZE.

THERE FOLLOWS A BRIEF PAUSE. THEN A DISTANT DOG CHIRPS AND OUR HEROES GO NO-WHERE. A BIG FAT NOTHING HAPPENS! BUT DO THEY NOTICE?

HMMM! IT LOOKS LIKE NOTHING HAPPENED.

SHE'S RIGHT!

53

Mikey is right. There is something strange happening here and I know what it is. Narrators know lots of stuff like this.

This maze is made from Vanadian granite, hewn from the craggy mountains of Vanadia in deepest dark bald Allo Peshia. It has curious and powerful magnetic qualities. Most importantly for our heroes, space/time travel devices like M.I.T. are absolutely useless around Vanadian granite. They will not work. Not even a tiny bit.

So there!

But the Ithacans don't know that.

'OK,' says Mikey. 'If the M.I.T. won't work here, we'll just have to defeat the maze using our brains.'

Interesting idea.

12

'Follow me,' says Claudia, leading them forward
in her crash-and-burn, this-maze-will-bend-to-my-
will approach. This gets them a little way into the
maze. But later, when they pass the statue of
Apollo for the fifth time, they realise the maze has
beaten them. The score is *Maze 1: Ithacans 0.*

Somehow they manage to find their way
out again. Mikey sits down to think through a
new strategy, while Claudia and Nico stand at
the entrance arguing about whose fault all of
this is.

'I've got it,' yells Mikey, leaping towards them.
'We each place one hand on the wall and never
take it off. If we walk for long enough we must get
to the centre.'

Claudia thinks for a while and sees the logic of
this idea. Nico just shrugs his shoulders and goes
along with it.

'Sounds cool to me. Let's go.'

They rush into the maze, keen to try out the
new theory. Twenty minutes later their enthusiasm
is flagging. Another twenty minutes later their
enthusiasm dies. *Maze 2: Ithacans 0.*

Mikey's idea was right. Keeping one hand on

the wall will eventually get you through any normal maze. But this is no normal maze.

The Ithacans try many other ideas but the scoreline blows out. *Maze 23: Ithacans 0.*

Nico comes up with a novel approach. He wants to climb the walls and run along the top to the centre. But each time he gets onto the wall, the mist descends and he cannot see where he is going. Nico gives up on this strategy after he gets confused and topples off the wall for the third time.

Mikey sits down again at the entrance to the maze.

'There must be a way,' he thinks. 'And how come every time we get lost and give up we easily find our way out of the maze?'

'Maybe there is some computer-type program that is always one step ahead of us, silently shifting the walls around to block our moves.'

'Maybe,' says Claudia.

'Follow me,' Mikey says, picking up a bit of chalky rock.

They walk into the maze, marking the wall as they go. After about five minutes they realise that they are getting no closer to the centre, and when Mikey turns back to look for the chalk marks on the wall, they are gone.

'There *is* some magic at work here, I am convinced of it,' he says.

'This is creepy,' says Nico. 'Let's get out of here.'

Mysteriously, they find their way out again very quickly.

By early afternoon, and probably two thousand strategies later, Nico has had enough.

'Why am I helping Claudia get to the centre of the maze anyway?' he wonders. 'She'll probably fall in love with that great lump of meat and forget me forever.'

'What are you muttering about, Nico?' says Claudia.

'I've had enough,' announces Nico. 'The surf is pounding. I'm off. Come on, M.I.T.'

M.I.T. leaps up into the nest of Nico's hair and they wander off to the beach.

'You can't leave me now,' Claudia yells after him. 'Quitter!'

'11011,' M.I.T. yells back.

13

HA! HA! HA! HA! Tricked you!!!

There is no Chapter 13!

HA! HA! HA! HA!

HA! HA! HA! HA!

HA! HA! HA! HA!

HA! HA! HA! HA!

HA! HA! HA! HA!

HA! HA! HA! HA!

14

Mikey watches Nico wander off to the beach and thinks he would rather be surfing too. But he feels for his poor love-struck friend, Claudia.

'There has to be a way,' says Mikey.

'I'm beginning to doubt that, Mikey.'

'That's got to be a first for you, Claudia.'

'Maybe Nico is right,' she says.

'We could try blind instinct,' says Mikey. 'Let's not think about it, let's just do it!'

'That might work,' says Claudia. 'Let me think about it.'

She does think about it for some time, and eventually Claudia decides that maybe Mikey is right. This is the time to throw away logic and put trust in natural impulses. So once again they walk through the entrance of the maze.

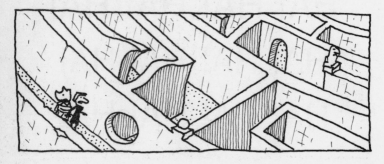

61

15

Claudia and Mikey sit on a large stone at the entrance to the maze.

'Any more ideas, Mikey?'

'No, this labyrinth has me defeated. We've tried every possible solution I've ever known and nothing seems to work.'

So the two Ithacans sit, leaning up against the stone wall in the misty gloom. Their eyelids grow heavy. They feel drowsy.

And they might well have fallen asleep, had Claudia not heard a faint sound.

'Listen, Mikey. Can you hear that?'

'What?'

'A voice.'

'Ah, yeah.'

'It's singing.'

'It's coming from up there,' says Mikey.

Up on the wall, in the gloom of an overhanging rock, hangs a spider's web. And in the middle of that spider's web sits a small spider.

Well, what did you expect? A horse?

Claudia and Mikey stand before the web, listening to the sweet sound of the spider's song. When I say sweet sound, I mean that the spider thinks it's sweet. To anybody else it sounds like fingernails being dragged down a blackboard. And it's not really a song. It's just the sound it makes when it spins its web. Spiders can't actually sing, or talk. Nor can horses.

And it's getting louder. **And louder.**
And louder!!!
'Stop!' says Claudia covering her ears.

But the spider doesn't stop. It is writing something in its web.

My name is Charlotte.

16

'Wow,' says Mikey. 'A talking spider... sort of.'

Claudia leans up really close to the spider. It isn't so special to look at. It has short fat little legs and dull grey skin and almost no distinguishing marks whatsoever... apart from a large red and green tattoo on its back of a heart and dagger with the word *Fang* written above it.

'Who are you?' Claudia asks. 'And what are you doing here? And how did you learn to write? And do you know the secret to this stupid maze?'

'And who is Fang?' asks Mikey.

The spider begins writing again. The thread slowly pours out of her rear end forming words on the web.

Slow down, 2 many Q?s. I only have 1 bum.

They make small talk for a while, until Claudia realises the spider is totally exhausted from writing. And there is one really important question that she wants to ask Charlotte.

'Can you tell us how to get to the centre of the Minotaur's maze?' Claudia asks.

Yes. Charlotte rests for a while.

But easier on my bum if I show you.

And why has Charlotte decided to help these strangers from another planet? Well, I can't tell you that yet. But she does have her reasons.

17

Back on the beach Nico prepares to hit the surf.

17

(Another one)

After a long rest, Charlotte stands with Claudia and Mikey at the entrance to the maze. She motions for them to step back while tying one end of her spider's thread to the wall. Then the high-pitched screeching starts again.

Anything happens to me, follow thread out. OK?

After writing that rather long sentence Charlotte has to take another long rest. She is rather an old spider, being over 112 in spider years. But I am not sure whether these are Ithacan spider years, Earth spider years or Knossus spider years. Nor is Mrs Narrator. And nor are you. So it doesn't matter.

'Nothing will happen to you, Charlotte,' says Claudia. 'We will protect you.'

☺, writes Charlotte.

Claudia and Mikey follow the spider into the maze. But their progress is slow as Charlotte has to stop every ten metres or so to rest her spinnerets in case they catch fire. Spinning thread is hot and exhausting work for an old spider.

18

Meanwhile Nico returns to the surf.

ON THE BEACH THE CEILING FAN IS MET BY A FLOCK OF AIRCONDITIONERS AND EVAPORATIVE COOLERS.

THEY GIVE HIM THE COLD SHOULDER.

THE CEILING FAN RUNS FROM THE BEACH.

HE TAKES REFUGE IN AN OLD RUBBISH TIP UNDER A CORRUGATED IRON LEAN-TO.

19

Welcome back to the maze, dear reader.

Progress is still slow.

PAINFULLY SLOW!!

Claudia and Mikey have travelled about five hundred metres and Charlotte is clearly becoming exhausted.

Mikey and Claudia have been forced to catch flies to keep Charlotte fuelled up. Unfortunately Mikey is hopeless at catching flies. But Claudia is a natural.

It helps being part lizard.

Suddenly Claudia turns around. 'What's that noise?'

There is a low drumming, breathing sort of sound that seems to be seeping out of the walls all around them.

'I have no idea,' says Mikey, 'but I don't like it.' His hands are becoming sweaty and he keeps a careful lookout ahead and behind.

'I have this feeling we are being watched,' whispers Claudia.

20

Must rest, writes Charlotte. She sits panting on the floor of the maze. Their progress has slowed to a spider's walk. Or maybe a spider's stagger.

And now the booming sound is even louder. They are almost overwhelmed by its breathing, footsteppy, heartbeaty, thumping presence. And every now and then Claudia and Mikey detect a smell like bad breath wafting around the walls of the maze.

'Stop farting, Mikey,' says Claudia.

'That's not me,' says Mikey. 'There's somebody or something all around us.'

Their minds flood with images from horror movies of people lost in misty mazes with all kinds of evil, slimy, squiddy, zomby, three-headed monsterish, gorgony, giant-squiddy, flesh-eating creatures following them and trying to feast on their entrails.

The mist seems to get thicker as they go further into the maze. Thicker and hotter and steamier. And now they are breathing harder and sweating freely. And the booming noise intensifies, like a really bad headache.

'Claudia, I don't like this,' says Mikey.
'We must keep going, Mikey.'
Don't give up. Nearly there.

21

And while Claudia and Mikey trudge through the steamy maze towards their inevitable doom, back on the beach, Nico surfs on.

MEANWHILE NOT FAR AWAY ON A HIGH ROCK WALL STANDS A LONELY, DEJECTED CEILING FAN. HIS LIFE IS AT ITS LOWEST POINT.

FOR MANY LONG MONTHS HE HAS ENDURED COLD,... LONELINESS, ACNE, BOILS...

AND OTHER HARDSHIPS TOO NUMEROUS TO MENTION.

SO, IT COMES TO THIS.

HE STANDS ON THE EDGE, READY TO THROW HIMSELF ON TO THE ROCKS BELOW. HE HEARS SOMETHING.

22

BOOM!
BOOOM!
BOOOOM!

Deep inside the maze noises boom all around Claudia, Mikey and Charlotte.

'Maybe it's Minotaur,' whispers Mikey.

☹, writes Charlotte.

Now there is howling as well as booming! This is too much for Mikey.

'I think we should turn back,' he says.

Claudia resists.

'We are so close, Mikey. We can't turn back now. I must meet him.'

Close.

'CCCCAAAAHH HHHWWWWW!!!'

'It's Minotaur!' yells Mikey as dark shapes rush towards him out of the misty gloom.

'Crows!' yells Claudia, dodging the swooping creatures. 'They're just crows, Mikey.'

'I hate crows,' he says, running away.

23

Suddenly they crash into a wall, stagger around a corner and stumble into an open space.

The booming stops.

Mikey and Claudia hold their breath and look around.

Here!

Claudia is disappointed. This is not what she was expecting at the centre of the maze. There is no man of her dreams standing here ready to be swept off his feet. There is no one here but them.

And an eerie silence.

'So where is he?' Claudia whispers.

'AAAR RRGGG HHH!!'

Minotaur leaps towards them. He stands over Claudia and Mikey, tall and threatening, his teeth bared in an evil snarl and drool dribbling from his lips.

He moves towards them. Mikey and Claudia shrink away back into the maze. Minotaur follows, growling and grimacing and pawing at the ground like a bull about to charge.

'Let's get out of here,' whispers Mikey.

But there is no way out. The beast has them cornered. He stands up to his full height and reaches out for Claudia.

24

'Hi, everybody!'

'**UUURRKK??**' Minotaur stops and turns around to face the new invader.

But this is no invader. It is Nico.

'Who are you?' the angry beast grunts, lurching at Nico. He grabs him by the neck and lifts him up. Minotaur would have throttled Nico and torn out his entrails right then and there. But fortunately somebody was following Nico into the maze.

'**Minotaur!** Stop that. Put him down, you big bully.'

'Ariadne,' he says surprised. 'What is going on?'

'Just put him down,' she says. 'This one is my friend.'

Friend? That's news to Nico. But this is not the time to argue.

Minotaur gently places Nico on the ground.

'Nico is brilliant,' says Ariadne.

'Brilliant?' laughs Claudia.

'Yes, brilliant! He found his way into the maze all by himself. With no help from anyone.'

91

They all look down on the crushed and pulverised body of Charlotte. A mist of silence descends over them all.

Charlotte's spirit leaves her body and floats up through the mist. Nico's foot has released her from the half-life she has been living on Knossus.

The selfless act of leading the Ithacans through the maze was the final good deed Charlotte needed to do. Now she is freed from the physical world. The gods grant her instant entry into the Heavenly Realm.

She has been waiting for someone like Nico to free her from the bonds of her mortal life for years. Farewell, Charlotte. Thank you, Nico.

25

'Ariadne, who are these people?' Minotaur asks. 'And what are they doing in MY maze?'

'Chill out, freak!' says Ariadne. 'What's the problem? Too much attention?'

'OK, don't bite my head off, Ari. What do they want?'

'Listen, swamp-breath, they are here to break you out.'

'Break me out? Why?'

'The tall ugly one is seriously loony. She thinks she is in love with you.'

'Love! Oh, dear!' says Minotaur, suddenly unsure of himself. He even blushes a little.

Claudia steps forward.

'I am Claudia from Ithaca and I have battled my way through this maze to find you, Minotaur. And now I'm going to release you from your prison and take you home with me.'

'But why?'

'Because you are the most gorgeous hunk of manhood I have ever set eyes on.'

Ariadne snorts. 'Give me a break!'

'You're crazy!' says Minotaur. 'I am a monster.'

'You are no monster,' says Claudia.

'Don't you believe it,' mutters Ariadne.

'He does look like a monster,' says Nico.

'The monkey-man is right. I am a monster and I will kill you all.'

'Grow up, Minotaur,' says Ariadne. 'You're a big pussy cat. You couldn't even kill time!'

'OK, Ari, maybe I won't kill them, but Father surely will when he discovers they are here.'

'Great Galloping Gorgons!' says Ariadne. 'The guards might be watching!' She points up to a security camera set high on the wall. 'We must move back into the maze.'

Actually, she needn't worry too much about the security. The two guards are Derek and Gordon, fugitives from far-off Duryllium. They talked their way into this job, but frankly they are not very good at it. But as Minotaur has not tried to escape since childhood, it hasn't mattered.

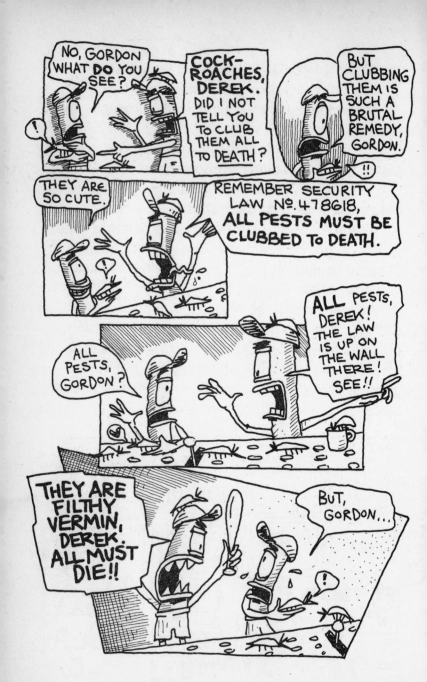

97

26

'You poor baby,' says Claudia. 'It must be horrible spending your whole life locked up in here.'

'Horrible? Oh no, it's great,' says Minotaur. 'I get three meals a day and they make my bed, clean my room. The guards even do my homework. Not very well, mind you.'

'But haven't you ever tried to escape?'

'I did when I was a little kid. I tried everything. Disguises, costumes, ropes, ladders, cannons, tunnels. But nothing worked. In the end, I gave up. Now I've grown to like it. It's MY maze. I have everything I ask for instantly brought to me. I'm on the Web. I have an unlimited supply of hair gel. What more could a Minotaur want?'

'But, Minotaur,' pleads Claudia. 'I can take you away from this misty shadowless world. You can experience the sunshine. You can be free to wander wherever you like. We can sit together watching the sunset.'

'Sunshine, eh?'

'Yes, Minotaur, it's time to embrace the big world outside your tiny maze.'

'Hmmmm,' thinks Minotaur, looking a bit worried. 'It's a BIG world out there, is it? Maybe it's too big, Clarissa?'

'CLAUDIA!!' she corrects him.

'Anyway it will never work,' says Minotaur. 'You're forgetting I am a freak. A real head-turning baby-scaring monster. My father is ashamed of me. He doesn't want anyone to see me. Ever.'

'He's not the only one!' hisses Ariadne.

'But that's so unfair,' says Clarissa. [Oops, I mean Claudia.]

'But he's doing it for my own good,' says Minotaur. 'Out in the big world, people will throw stones at me. They'll lock me up. Or worse, turn me into a freak show and put me on TV. I am a beast. I will always be a beast.'

'Have you ever heard the story of the Ugly Duckling?' Claudia asks Minotaur.

'The ugly what?'

'Duckling.'

'Nope. I've never heard that one.'

Claudia tells him the story. I am sure you, dear reader, will have heard this story many times, so I am not going to repeat it here. Nor am I going to show you a stick-figure version. We just don't have time. Go and look it up in your school library. And if you don't have a school library, go ask your teacher. And if you don't have a teacher, go ask a duck.

Minotaur loves the story.

'So I'm just like the big swan,' he says.

'A big goose, more likely,' says Ariadne.

'Got it in one,' Nico agrees.

'You are not a beast, Minotaur,' Claudia continues, ignoring the others. 'Do you think *I* would ever fall in love with a beast? Do you? I don't think so.'

'Love?' muses Minotaur.

This discussion is starting to go well beyond his limited experience. He is looking confused. Ariadne realises she must seize this moment. If she can convince Minotaur to go with Claudia, she might be rid of him forever. No longer will she have to put up with the constant, 'Is poor Minotaur OK?' and 'Should we get Minotaur this?' or 'Poor lonely Minotaur needs that.' She might get some love and attention for a change.

'She's right, Mini,' says Ariadne.

'Mini?' Nico sniggers.

'You are not a monster, Mini. I know you too well. You are gentle and sensitive and strong and intelligent.'

'Gee, thanks Ari.'

Ariadne can't believe she is saying this to the big, dumb baboon. But the job's not done yet.

'You are my brother, Mini, and, of course, I would miss you. But you must leave here for your own good.'

'But this is my home, Ari. I would miss you all . . . '

'You great thick-head,' Ariadne interrupts. 'Don't you see, if you stay here, you WILL become a monster. You need to get away and rebuild your life. Become a real person, not some glorified guinea-pig. Then one day you can return home and show Father you are not a monster. Then he will accept you!'

'Then,' Ariadne thinks, 'you can rack off again and I will have Father all to myself!'

As you may have guessed, dear reader, Ariadne is seriously loony.

Now she looks her brother in the eye.

'You must escape. You must go at once.'

'If you say so, Ari,' says Minotaur. 'You know I'd do anything for you.'

Mikey takes Claudia aside.

'Are you sure about this Minotaur? Maybe he has been locked up too long. He might be a bit weird.'

Claudia scoffs at Mikey.

'Jealousy, Mikey,' she says. 'You men are hopeless.'

Then she turns to Minotaur.

'OK, you great piece of Murillion tofu. This is your big chance to see the world. Are you in or out?'

'I'm out,' he says proudly.

'**Out?!!**' Claudia and Ariadne shout together.

'I mean I want to go out. Out of the maze,' Minotaur explains rather sheepishly.

'Brilliant!' says Claudia.

'Brilliant!!' thinks Ariadne.

27

'But how are we going to escape from here?' asks Mikey. 'Nico rolled up Charlotte's thread.'

'Don't remind me of that,' says Claudia.

'And he stomped on Charlotte,' adds Mikey.

'Or that,' says Claudia.

'Is there any other way out, Ariadne?'

'Not really. The tunnel is too well guarded. The maze is the only way out.'

'We could try M.I.T.,' says Mikey.

'M.I.T.?' asks Ariadne. 'What's that?'

'This is M.I.T.,' says Nico as the small biomorph emerges out of the nest of his hair.

'11000.'

'Oh, Nico,' says Ariadne, 'you are SO clever.'

'He is a space/time travel device,' says Nico. 'He can take us any place any time in the universe.'

'Only he's not very good at it,' grunts Claudia.

'11011.'

'Oh. A space/time travel device,' says Ariadne. 'Your M.I.T. won't work in this maze, then. It is built with Vanadian granite.'

'The M.I.T. is?' squeaks Nico in surprise.

'No, she means the maze, you pin-head,' explains Claudia.

'All space/time travel devices are powerless around Vanadian granite,' says Ariadne. 'Away from the maze your M.I.T. might work OK, but in here he is useless.'

KLUNK!

That is the sound of a gloom descending on the whole group.

'Then we're trapped in here,' says Claudia. 'And when King Minos discovers us, we're dead.'

'He'll go ballistic,' says Minotaur. 'He'll tear you apart and feed your entrails to the wolves. He loves doing that.'

'Why do they always want to feed our entrails to wolves?' asks Nico. 'Why do dogs like entrails so much?'

'Father will be angry,' says Ariadne, slyly. 'I may be able to calm him and beg him for mercy. But he will imprison you all, probably somewhere in the health farm.'

'Locked up in a health farm for the rest of our lives,' yell Mikey and Nico. **'No more Haggis Burgers! No more Gorgon Cola! NO MORE SURF!!! We'd rather die!'**

'I am sure you will,' says Minotaur. 'There's no way we will be able to calm Father down enough to save you.'

KLUNK!

More gloom!

'And to think,' says Claudia, taking Minotaur by the arm. 'Just yesterday I had romantic dreams of lifting you up and flying you out of here. What was I thinking?'

'Ha. Ha. What an idiot!' says Nico. 'Fly him out of here. Claudia, you hopeless romantic.'

'Maybe that's it!' yells Mikey.

'That's what?' says Nico.

'We fly out of here,' says Mikey. 'Just like Icarus and Daedalus.'

'Ica-what?'

'The Legend of Icarus,' says Mikey. 'You know.'

'No,' says Nico.

'The ancient Greek myth!'

'Sorry, doesn't compute.'

'Don't worry. The important thing is that we don't have to go through the maze. We can go over the maze. We can **fly** out of here.'

Mikey, Nico, Claudia and Ariadne sit around the rock table and after half an hour they devise a plan.

Ariadne sets off down the tunnel with a list of technical requirements, known as stuff. And a list of food.

'We cannot perform great deeds on empty stomachs,' a great friend once said. Actually she was the beautiful goddess, Diarrhoea, God of Plenty. I met her once when I was young and foolish. We spent many happy hours together on one of the moons of Uranus. Oh, yes, one sloppy tale.

But that's another story.

28

Ariadne passes through the security door, which instantly recognises her genetic code.

But when she walks through the tunnel and into the Security Control Booth, the guards are confused.

'Do you remember us letting Ariadne in, Gordon?' Derek asks.

'I don't remember anything after you hit me with that club, Derek,' says Gordon.

'I was only trying to kill the cockroaches, Gordon.'

'That was no cockroach, Derek. That was my head!'

'Excuse me,' says Ariadne. 'But I have a list of stuff here that Minotaur needs.'

'Stuff?' says Derek. 'What kind of stuff?'

'Stuff to build a sunshade. And he wants it today, so you'd better get moving. We wouldn't want to keep precious old Minotaur waiting, would we?'

'Certainly, Miss Ariadne,' says Gordon, who is more than happy to help because, I'll let you in on a secret, he fancies her.

Derek takes a look at the list.

'Hmmm, I don't think this will be possible,' he says. 'King Minos would not approve.'

'**YOU** don't think so, Derek?' says Gordon, still nursing his aching head. '**YOU?** Is it not **ME** who makes the decisions around here? Did King Minos not give me that responsibility, Derek?'

'But, Gordon, thirty metres of sailcloth and twenty carbon-fibre poles?!! That sounds suspicious to me.'

'Oh, it sounds suspicious to you does it, Derek?'

'And a whole barrel of wax-glue,' adds Derek. 'Very suspicious, indeed.'

'And what do you think he is up to, Derek?'

'I think he is going to make some wings and try to fly out of the maze, Gordon,' says Derek. 'And I won't allow it.'

'**YOU** won't allow it. Let me remind you who is in charge here, Derek.'

'But, King Minos said...'

'Enough, Derek! I make the decisions around here. And I am sure that Master Minotaur has no plans for escape. Is that right, Mistress Ariadne?'

Ariadne nods agreement. 'He's just building a sunshade. That's all.'

'A sunshade? But, Gordon, there is no sun in...'

'Silence, Derek. My mind is made up. Fetch the stuff. And that's an end to it.'

'Oh, I nearly forgot,' says Ariadne. 'He is very hungry, too.'

'Yes, Mistress.'

'VERY hungry indeed. Bring him enough food to feed four people.'

'1101.'

'Make that four and a half people.'

'Certainly, Mistress Ariadne.'

'And get yourselves a couple of bottles of the finest Snake Oil, boys.'

Snake Oil is a very popular alcoholic beverage on Knossus. It is made from the fermented eggs of Mambo snakes. Very tasty indeed.

108

29

Ariadne returns to the maze some time later with Derek and Gordon carrying all the food and equipment.

'Where do you want this, Mr Minotaur?' asks Gordon.

'Just on the table.'

'Do you need a hand putting all this together, Mr Minotaur?'

'No,' replies Minotaur. 'I've got plenty of help.'

'Help?' says Derek, looking around.

'He means me,' says Ariadne. 'You can go.'

Derek and Gordon retire to their Security Booth.

'Pour me out some Snake Oil, Derek,' says Gordon.

'Do you think we should?'

Gordon surveys the Security Monitors.

'All is quiet, Derek. I think we can risk it.'

Later that night Ariadne creeps down the tunnel. She slips past the gaggle of sensors and alarms which recognise her genetic code and she silently opens the door of the Security Booth.

Derek and Gordon are asleep at their consoles. Ariadne tip-toes past them and reaches into their storage cupboard. She takes out an old security tape and returns to the console. She reaches over Gordon and ejects the recording tape. She then places the old tape in the player.

As she pulls her elbow back, she accidentally knocks over a glass of Snake Oil.

Gordon stirs. He reaches out in his sleep and takes hold of Ariadne's arm.

'My lovely,' he purrs. 'My lovely.'

Ariadne stands absolutely still. Afraid to move in case she wakes Gordon. But eventually he subsides back into a deep sleep.

Working quickly, Ariadne pushes the old tape into the player and presses the 'repeat-play' button.

Now it won't matter if the guards wake. Derek and Gordon will think everything is normal, as the monitors will show Minotaur asleep on his bed in the centre of the maze. In their drunken state they will not realise they are watching an old tape.

Her job done, Ariadne slips out of the Security Booth and joins her brother and his friends in the maze.

30

With no fear that they will be discovered, the Ithacans, Minotaur and Ariadne begin building their wings. Mikey oversees the work, much to Claudia's annoyance.

They trim and join the poles together. Then they cut the sailcloth and wax-glue it to the poles. In just a few hours they have built four sets of hang-glider wings, and a smaller fifth set for M.I.T.

'Nico,' says Minotaur, 'your edges are very messy. Would you like me to clean them up?'

'No, they are fine!'

'I tell you, they will fall apart. Look at mine.'

'He'll be OK, Minotaur,' says Mikey.

'Well, **he** might be,' says Minotaur, 'but you won't. Your wings are cut all wrong.'

'What?'

'Look at mine,' says Minotaur. 'Parabolic wings! With my superior weight-to-strength ratio they will give me more lift and more power than yours. You won't get off the ground with those.'

'We'll see,' says Mikey.

A little while later, Nico and Mikey are working together, gluing M.I.T.'s wings.

Nico whispers, nodding towards Minotaur, 'He IS a monster!'

'Yeah,' says Mikey. 'Maybe he's just been locked up on his own too long. He is used to doing things HIS way. Just don't let him get under your skin, Nico.'

When they are finished building all the wings, they carry them back into the maze a little way to hide them from the security cameras.

'Now it's way past my bedtime,' says Minotaur. 'I need some sleep,'

'In the morning,' says Ariadne, 'the breeze should blow in from the sea. It's usually strong. It should lift us up and out of here.'

'Then with my mighty parabolic wings,' says Minotaur, 'I shall soar highest and fastest of us all. I will lead us to freedom.'

'I think I'm going to be sick!' whispers Nico.

'Me, too,' says Ariadne.

31

32

As M.I.T. returns to the maze and drops down through the mist, he calls out to Nico.

'00111.'

'Look, everyone,' says Nico, 'M.I.T. is flying.'

Quickly the others strap on their wings and climb up on the various rocks and tables and hold out their wings trying to catch the wind.

But they soon realise they are much heavier than M.I.T. and the breeze is far too light to lift them up.

Then the wind drops away altogether.
They are forced to spend the rest of the day sitting around waiting for the wind to return.

Claudia and Minotaur sit together talking.
He tells her stories of his deeds of endurance and mental strength and of his cunning in outsmarting his guards and his father. I won't bore you with the details. Nico and Mikey are bored with the details, but Claudia is fascinated.

'He's so into himself,' whispers Nico. 'Just like Claudia.'

'Much worse,' says Mikey.

'Does he ever shut up about how wonderful he is?'

'When he's asleep,' replies Mikey.

'No,' adds Ariadne. 'Even in his sleep, he brags endlessly.'

'I need a distraction,' says Nico. 'Cooped up in here much longer, I'll...'

'You and I could go for a walk in the maze,' suggests Ariadne.

'What about MORE FOOD?' suggests Mikey, suddenly getting excited.

'Good idea, Mikey.' Nico turns to Ariadne. 'Let's eat.'

'Yes, OK,' says Ariadne. 'I'll go order some tucker, then.'

33

Ariadne goes back through the tunnel to the Security Booth, where Derek and Gordon are still sleeping soundly. Given the amount of Snake Oil they drank last night they are lucky to be alive.

Ariadne is easily able to switch security tapes and place the old one back in the cupboard. Then she has great fun waking up Derek and Gordon. I'll spare you the details, because I don't want to die of old age telling this story, but they are most embarrassed at being caught asleep on duty and beg Ariadne not to tell King Minos.

She reassures them and sends them off to fill Minotaur's food order.

In the kitchen, Derek reads the food order and starts to wonder.

'Young Mr Minotaur is eating a lot, is he not, Gordon?' asks Derek.

'Quiet, Derek!' whispers Gordon. 'My head is still pounding from that Snake Oil.'

'Perhaps he is still a growing boy,' Derek wonders out loud.

'Maybe our young master is not well,' groans Gordon.

'Perhaps worms are nibbling at his entrails, Gordon,' suggests Derek.

'I think I should tell King Minos,' says Gordon.
'Wait for me,' says Derek.

Ariadne is sitting at the consoles when King
Minos and Derek and Gordon burst into the
Security Control Booth.

'These two say that Minotaur is feeling unwell,'
says Minos to Ariadne.
'Indeed I do, Master,' says Derek.
'**YOU** do, Derek?' says Gordon. 'Master, it was
ME who became suspicious first. Minotaur is
eating enough for four people.'
'Four and a half,' adds Derek.
'Either he is sick or...'
'Or there is someone else in the maze with
him,' says King Minos.

'Oh, there's no one else in the maze, Master,' says Gordon. 'We haven't taken our eyes off – '

'Silence, you fool!' commands Minos. 'What do you think, Ariadne?'

'As usual, you are worrying about him too much, Father. He's just a growing boy.'

'What about those Ithacans?' asks Minos. 'They didn't turn up for their Brussels Sprout Enemas this morning. And they have been acting suspiciously. Maybe they found their way into the maze.'

'It's impossible,' says Ariadne, moving to stand directly in front of the monitor trained on the centre of the maze.

'Maybe someone helped them,' says Minos.

'Why would anyone want to do that?' asks Ariadne, as she fidgets with her necklace. But she fidgets too hard and her necklace breaks. Beads fall and bounce all over the floor. Ariadne bends to catch them and Minos is left staring straight at Minotaur on the TV, playing with his wings.

'They are in the maze. And they've got wings!'

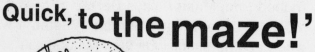

Quick, to the maze!'

34

DDDWWWEEEE!!!
BBBBAAARRRPPPP!
HHHOOOWWWLLL!!!
WWWEEEE!!!
WWWWAAAAA!!!
WWWWEEEEE!!!
WWWWAAA!!!

The sensors overload and all the alarms go off as King Minos and the guards storm into the centre of the maze, surrounding Minotaur and the Ithacans.

'Minotaur, take off those ridiculous wings,' King Minos demands.

'No, Father, I have had enough of being cooped up in my labyrinth,' Minotaur replies.

'What's a labyrinth again, Mikey?' whispers Nico.

'Quiet, idiot!' hisses Claudia.

'But it's for your own good,' says Minos. 'You cannot survive in the outside world. People will destroy you when they see you.'

'Because I am ugly?'

King Minos nods, a tear coming to his eye.

'But, Father, haven't you heard the story of the Ugly Duckling?' asks Minotaur.

'The what?'

'Surely you know it, Father?'

'No,' says Minos. 'I've heard of Roast Duckling, Steamed Duckling, Sweet and Sour Duckling but never Ugly Duckling.'

'Well, let me see, how does it go?' says Minotaur. 'Once upon a time there was this duckling who lived with other ducks. They don't like him much and pick on him and if they had a maze they would have locked him up in it. And eventually he turns into a really, really big goose. And they live happily ever after.'

'I think we know who the big goose is here!' whispers Ariadne.

'Enough about ducks and geese, Minotaur,' shouts King Minos. 'You're not going anywhere. Guards! Remove their wings!'

King Minos's guards move towards Minotaur. But he runs away from them and leaps up on to the big stone table.

'You'll never catch me alive,' says he, leaping at the wall. It is a desperate attempt to escape. Doomed to failure.

But at that very moment, as if the gods will it, the wind blows hard and catches under Minotaur's parabolic wings. Slowly he rises above the maze and floats up through the mist. The Ithacans and M.I.T. leap into the air and follow Minotaur up through the mist.

'Come back, Minotaur,' calls his father. 'You will bring shame on us all.'

King Minos reaches into his pocket and takes out his extra long acupuncture needles. He looks up towards his fast disappearing son and takes aim.

He hesitates.

'Let him go, Father,' Ariadne whispers in his ear. 'He has a right to his own life. And anyway you've still got me!'

King Minos looks up at his hideously ugly son and slowly lowers the acupuncture needles. He watches as his Minotaur drifts further up through the veil of mist and out of his sight forever.

35

The Ithacans and Minotaur fly up high above the health farm and soon the island is just a tiny speck in the distance. Although I should point out the island has not turned into a tiny speck. It is as big as it ever was. But because they have flown a long way away from it, the island appears very small. I just thought you should know that.

Minotaur looks around. For the first time in his life he looks at the clean, crisp blue sky.

'Wow, no mist!'

And for the first time in his life he laughs.

Then Minotaur looks down.

'AAAARRRGGGHHH!!! What if I crash,' he yells, suddenly aware he is up so high. 'That looks like water below and I can't swim.'

'And I thought you could do everything,' says Nico.

'You won't crash,' says Claudia. 'And even if you did, I would rescue you. Stay close to me and don't look down and you won't get scared.'

Calmed by Claudia, Minotaur looks up again at the sun.

For the second time in his life he laughs.

'WOW! That thing is brilliant,' he shouts.

'The sun?' asks Claudia.

'Yes. It is hot,' says Minotaur turning to look back at Claudia. 'Just like you.'

Claudia blushes.

Nico gags.

'You have nothing to worry about,' Mikey warns Minotaur. 'As long as you don't soar too high.'

'Too high?'

'If you fly too close to the sun, it's heat will melt the wax-glue in your wings.'

'Wax-glue? These things are held together by wax? What are you trying to do to me?'

'Don't worry,' says Claudia. 'Just stick close by me and you'll be OK.'

Minotaur is happy to stay beside Claudia for the moment. Sometimes he stares at her. But more and more he looks up at the sun. He is dazzled by its brilliance and by the brilliance of all the colours of the sky, the sea, his clothes and his wings. He has never seen such vivid colours in his life.

Can you imagine what it would be like coming from a dull grey world and seeing sunshine and colours for the first time? No? Well, nor can I. But I'm asking you to try, because that's what Minotaur is experiencing right now.

36

'We must find somewhere to land,' says Mikey.
'Then we can take off these wings and use M.I.T.
to get back home.'

'Look,' says Claudia, pointing below. 'That
island looks uninhabited.'

'Perfect.'

They descend towards the island, but Minotaur
hangs back. He hovers above them, watching
Claudia. And then he looks back up at the sun. Its
brilliance overwhelms him.

Again he looks back down to Claudia. Then
once more he looks upward to the sun as if in his
mind he is weighing up some difficult choice.

THE HEAT OF THE SUN MELTS THE WAX-GLUE HOLDING MINOTAUR'S WINGS TOGETHER.

SUDDENLY THE MATERIAL PEELS OFF.

FLAP!

UH, OH.

FLAP!

FLAP!

AARR GGHH!!

37

'**MINOTAUR!!**' yells Claudia, suddenly realising he is no longer with them. **'Where is Minotaur?'**

They look all around but can't see him anywhere in the sky.

'Look down there, in the sea,' says Nico.

Floating in the water below them are torn pieces of sailcloth and a few poles. But there is no sign of Minotaur. And if you were listening before you would have heard me mention that he can't swim.

So that must be the end of him.

And also there is a school of white pointer sharks swimming around close by.

And a pod of killer dolphins.

And a huge school of
man-eating sardines.
And an Axis of
Evil spy submarine.
So he's dead!
OK!!!

38

'Did we do the right thing, Mikey?' says Claudia.

'Eh?'

'Breaking Minotaur out of his maze? He was comfortable there. Safe. But I had to fall in love with him, didn't I?'

'Call that love?' says Nico quietly.

'That's life, Claudia,' says Mikey.

'I had to try and give him a taste of freedom. Release him into the big wide world.'

'But, that's life.'

'He wasn't ready for it, Mikey.'

'Yeah, but that's life,' says Mikey.

'And that freedom and my love killed him.'

'Yeah, well, that's death.'

131

'Now I wish I'd never met him,' says Claudia. 'And yet I'm so glad I did.'

'Now, that's confusing,' says Mikey.

'That's life!' says Nico.

39

OK, that's it.

Time to pack the book away and go off and clean up your room, do your homework or pay attention to your teacher or whatever. And I must go, too.

Our story is over, more or less.

Nico, Mikey and Claudia have returned safely to Ithaca. Claudia misses her Minotaur and so she is heartbroken. Nico's heart is broken because Claudia's heart is broken over Minotaur. And Mikey's heart is still broken from the last story.

And on Knossus, Ariadne's heart is broken because she loves Nico. Poor misguided girl! And King Minos's heart is broken because he believes he will never see his beloved son again. So Ariadne's heart is double-broken because her father is too busy mourning Minotaur to care about her.

The universe is littered with broken hearts. If you know a good heart doctor, there's a small fortune to be made on Ithaca and Knossus.

And what of M.I.T.? Well he's the only one who doesn't have a broken heart.

But that's possibly because he is a genetically engineered biomorph and doesn't have a heart to break. So they say.

And meanwhile, the cause of all this heartbreak, the ugly duckling Minotaur, slips out of our lives forever.

Or does he?

40

A GUIDE TO M.I.T.'S* LANGUAGE

1	I hate surfing
0	There's lice in here!
00	I'm too young to die
01	You idiot!
10	I hate sand
11	Bummer
000	Oh, OH!
001	OH, NO!
010	Hello
011	Goodnight
100	Welcome back, goanna-head
101	Pooh!
110	Ouch!
111	ZZZZZ
0000	My yak has fleas
0001	HELP!
0010	Oh, joy
0011	Go away
0100	That's handy
0101	You double idiot
0110	Why me?
0111	And two hard-boiled eggs
1000	Hee hee
1001	This is another fine mess
1010	I'm not coming out
1011	His feet stink
1100	What about my TV?
1101	What about me?
1111	I'm outta here
00000	My head hurts
00001	It's not my fault
00011	That would hurt
00100	This is nice!
00101	This is serious!

00110	The roof is leaking
00111	Hello, ugly!
01001	Hold my hand
01010	Can't make me
01100	Not telling
01101	What's this?
01110	Bye, bye
01111	GRRRR!
10001	Die, you fiend!
10010	Get this smelly lump off me
10101	Just following orders
10111	Panic stations!
11000	Hello, strange animal-headed people
11011	Smarter than you, lizard-brains
11111	HEE HEE HEE
100000	It's only a flesh wound
100011	I want my mummy
100101	Just following orders, fly-breath
100111	Quiet, you stupid animal-headed people
101001	Can't catch me!
101010	Put me down!
101100	Let me go!
101110	What the @%£#$* am I doing here?
110001	You smell, lizard-brains!
110010	Holy Occhilupo, you're ugly
110011	Get your bottom off my leg
110101	Holy Occhilupo!
110110	Gulp!
110111	The whole world's turned dark
111001	My feet are on fire
111010	I hate water
111011	@%&#$*!!
111100	NNNOOO!
111101	The kettle's boiling
1110111	Yes!

*M.I.T. (pronounced *em-eye-tee*) is short for Mental Image Transfer.

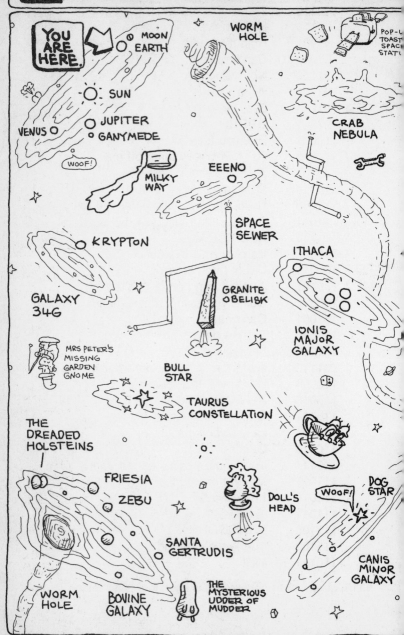

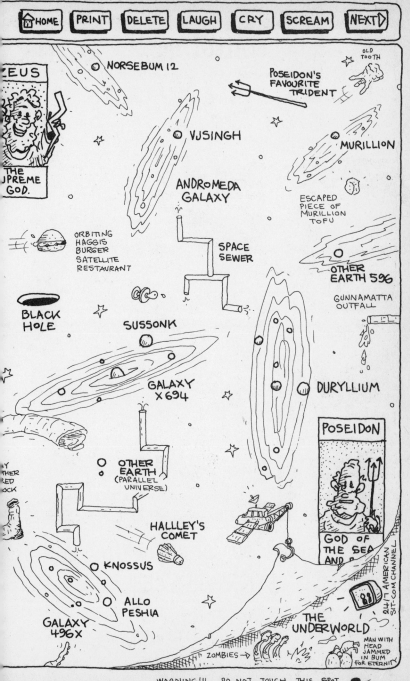

COLLECT THE
STORYMAZE
SERIES!

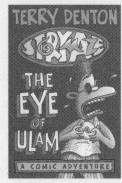

Look out for the next
STORYMAZE
adventure!